MW00478137

OPERA JOURNEYS LIBRETTO SERIES

Gaetano Donizetti's

LUCIA DI LAMMERMOOR

COMPLETE LIBRETTO
with Music Highlight examples

Edited by Burton D. Fisher
Principal lecturer, *Opera Journeys Lecture Series*

Opera Journeys Publishing™ / Coral Gables, Florida

WEB SITE: www.operajourneys.com   E MAIL: operaj@bellsouth.net

Libretto

LUCIA DI LAMMERMOOR

Act I
Act II

Act 1 - Scene 1

THE DEPARTURE

On the grounds of the Ravenswood Castle.
Norman, the Captain of the Ravenswood Guard, and retainers appear,
all wearing hunting attire.

Normanno e Coro:
Percorrete le spiagge vicine,
percorriamo della torre le vaste rovine:
cada il velo di sì turpe mistero,
lo domanda, lo impone l'onor.
Splenderà l'esecrabile vero
come lampo fra nubi d'orror!

Norman and Chorus:
Search the nearby beaches,
and let's search the ruins of the old tower:
let's solve this mystery,
because our honor demands it.
Let the awful truth be revealed
like a flash of lightning!

After the retainers depart, Norman approaches Lord Henry Ashton.

Normanno:
Tu sei turbato!

Norman:
You seem troubled!

Enrico:
E n'ho ben donde.
Il sai: del mio destin si ottenebrò la stella.
Intanto Edgardo, quel mortal nemico
di mia prosapia, dalle sue rovine
erge la fronte baldanzosa e ride!
Sola una mano raffermar mi puote
nel vacillante mio poter.
Lucia osa respinger quella mano!
Ah! Suora non m'è colei!

Henry: *(disdainfully)*
I have reason to be.
My entire future is in danger.
And Edgar, my family's mortal enemy,
mocks me, haughtily sitting
in his crumbling castle and laughing at me!
Only one man
can help me regain power.
But Lucy refuses to marry him.
She's no longer my sister!

Raimondo:
Dolente Vergin, che geme sull'urna recente
di cara madre, al talamo potria
volger lo sguardo?
Ah! Rispettiam quel core che per troppo
dolor non sente amore.

Raymond: *(trying to be conciliatory)*
The poor girl is still mourning her beloved
mother. At this time, how can she think of
love or marriage?
Let's respect her grief. Her heart is too
burdened with sadness to think of love.

Normanno:
Schivo d'amor!
Lucia d'amore avvampa.

Norman: *(ironically)*
Don't talk of love!
Lucy is inflamed with love!

Enrico:
Che favelli?

Henry:
What are you saying?

Raimondo:
(Oh detto!)

Normanno:
M'udite. Ella sen gìa colà, del parco nel
solingo vial dove la madre giace sepolta.
Impetuoso toro ecco su lor s'avventa,
quando per l'aria rimbombar si sente un
colpo, e al suol repente cade la belva.

Enrico:
E chi vibrò quel colpo?

Normanno:
Tal che il suo nome ricoprì d'un velo.

Enrico:
Lucia forse?

Normanno:
L'amò.

Enrico:
Dunque il rivide?

Normanno:
Ogni alba.

Enrico:
E dove?

Normanno:
In quel viale.

Enrico:
Io fremo! Né tu scovristi il seduttor?

Normanno:
Sospetto io n'ho soltanto.

Enrico:
Ah! Parla!

Normanno:
È tuo nemico.

Raimondo:
(Oh ciel!)

Raymond:
(Oh heavens!)

Norman:
Listen to me. She was walking a lonely path
in the park, where her mother is buried.
Suddenly, a wild boar rushed from a thicket
and charged at her. Then a shot rang through
the air, and the beast fell to the ground.

Henry:
Who fired the shot?

Norman:
I shouldn't mention his name.

Henry:
And what did Lucy do?

Norman:
She fell in love with him.

Henry:
Does she meet with him?

Norman:
Every morning.

Henry:
Where?

Norman:
In that alley.

Henry:
I tremble! Do you know the seducer's name?

Norman:
I only have a suspicion.

Henry:
Tell me!

Norman:
He's your enemy.

Raymond:
(Oh heavens!)

Normanno:
Tu lo detesti.

Norman:
You detest him.

Enrico:
Esser potrebbe Edgardo?

Henry:
Could it be Edgar?

Raimondo:
(Ah!)

Raymond:
(Ah!)

Normanno:
Lo dicesti.

Norman:
You named him yourself.

Larghetto
HENRY

Cru - da, fune - sta sma - nia   *tu m'hai svegliato in pet - to!*

Enrico:
Cruda funesta smania
tu m'hai svegliato in petto!
È troppo, è troppo orribile,
questo fatal sospetto!
Mi fa gelare e fremere,
solleva in fronte il crin! Ah!
Colma di tanto obbrobrio
chi suora a me nascea!
Ah! Pria che d'amor sì perfido
a me svelarti rea,
se ti colpisse un fulmine,
fora men rio dolor.

Henry:
What a cruel blow,
and what fury this arouses in me!
It is too horrible,
this dreadful suspicion!
It turns my heart to ice,
and incites my anger!
I renounced him
the moment he was born!
If my sister is guilty
of such a treacherous alliance,
may a thunderbolt
strike her down.

Normanno:
(Pietoso al tuo decoro, io fui con te crudel!)

Norman:
(I had to tell you the truth, however cruel it may be!)

Raimondo:
(La tua clemenza imploro;
tu lo smentisci, o ciel!)

Raymond:
(I implore your forgiveness,
oh heaven, don't let it be so!)

Coro:
Il tuo dubbio è omai certezza.

Chorus of Huntsmen: *(to Norman)*
Your worst fears have come true.

Normanno:
Odi tu?

Norman: *(to Henry)*
Did you hear?

Enrico:
Narrate.

Henry:
Tell me.

Raimondo:
(Oh giorno!)

Raymond:
(Oh, what a day!)

Chorus:
Come vinti da stanchezza,
dopo lungo errare intorno,
noi posammo della torre
nel vestibulo cadente:
ecco tosto lo trascorre
in silenzio un uom pallente.
Come appresso ei n'è venuto
ravvisiam lo sconosciuto:
ei su rapido destriero
s'involò dal nostro sguardo.
Qual s'appella un falconiero
ne apprendeva, qual s'appella.

Chorus:
We were exhausted
after taking so many false turns.
We rested in a courtyard
by the tower ruins.
There, in total silence,
a pale rider appeared.
As he came nearer,
we recognized him:
and he quickly galloped away,
and was out of our sight.
We met a falconer
who told us his name.

Enrico:
E quale?

Henry:
Who is he?

Chorus:
Edgardo.

Chorus:
Edgar.

Enrico:
Egli! Oh rabbia che m'accendi, contenerti
un cuor non può!

Henry:
Him! Fury is inflamed in me, and I can no
longer contain my heart!

Raimondo:
Ah! Non credere, no, no, deh sospendi.
ella. M'odi!

Raymond:
Don't believe it.
Listen to me!

Enrico:
Udir non vo'!

Henry:
I don't want to hear any more!

Allegretto moderato
HENRY

La pie-ta - de in suo fa - vor - re, mi-ti sen-si in - van mi det - ta.

La pietade in suo favore,
miti sensi invan mi detta.
Sì mi parli di vendetta
solo intenderti potrò.

It's useless
to speak to me of compassion.
I only understand
the language of revenge.

Sciagurati! Il mio furore
già su voi tremendo rugge
l'empia fiamma che vi strugge
io col sangue spegnerò.

Wretches! Let my fury
roar over them like a storm.
I'll extinguish the flames
of their passion with spilled blood.

Normanno, Coro:
Ti raffrena, al nuovo albore ei da te fuggir
non può.

Norman, Chorus:
Calm your wrath! He cannot escape, and he
will pay with his blood.

Raimondo:
(Ah! Qual nube di terrore.)
Questa casa circondò!)

Raymond:
(Ah! What a cloud of terror.
It will destroy your house!)

Act I - Scene 2

A park in the Castle gardens at Lammermoor. It is a moonlit evening.
In the background there is a gateway; in the foreground, a fountain.
Lucy Ashton arrives, followed by her companion, Alice.
Both are extremely agitated, looking about as if seeking someone.
When they see the fountain, they turn away from it, as if it harbors some mysterious curse.

Lucia:
Ancor non giunse!

Lucy:
He hasn't arrived yet!

Alisa:
Incauta! A che mi traggi?
Avventurarti, or che il fratel qui venne,
è folle ardir.

Alice:
Be careful! Where are you taking me?
This adventure is madness, fatal if your
brother should discover us.

Lucia:
Ben parli! Edgardo sappia qual ne circonda
orribile periglio.

Lucy:
I must warn Edgar that he's in terrible
danger.

Alisa:
Perché d'intorno il ciglio volgi atterrita?

Alice:
What are you staring at?

Lucia:
Quella fonte, ah, mai, senza tremar non
veggo.
Ah! Tu lo sai:
un Ravenswood, ardendo di geloso furor,
l'amata donna colà trafisse,
e l'infelice cadde nell'onda,
ed ivi rimanea sepolta.
M'apparve l'ombra sua.

Lucy:
That fountain, I tremble whenever I look at
it.
But you understand the reason:
once, long ago, a Ravenswood was
consumed by a jealous fury, and slew an
unfortunate woman right on this spot.
The poor girl fell into the water, and that is
where she is buried. I've seen her ghost.

Alisa:
Che dici!

Alice:
What are you saying!

Lucia:
Ascolta.

Lucy:
Listen.

Larghetto
LUCY

Regnava nel silenzio
alta la notte e bruna,
colpìa la fonte un pallido
raggio di tetra luna,
quando sommesso un gemito
fra l'aure udir sì fe',
ed ecco su quel margine,
l'ombra mostrarsi a me!

Everything was silent.
It was late, and the night was dark.
A pale ray of moonlight shone down on the
fountain.
Suddenly, I heard a stifled cry,
that seemed to float on the breeze.
And there at the fountain's edge,
her ghost appeared before me!

Qual di chi parla muoversi
il labbro suo vedea,
e con la mano esanime,
chiamarmi a sè parea;
stette un momento immobile,
poi ratta, dileguò,
e l'onda pria sì limpida
di sangue rosseggiò!

I could see her lips moving.
She tried to summon me
with her lifeless hand.
She stood there
motionless for a moment,
and then she vanished.
And the water, which had been so clear,
became red with blood!

Alisa:
Chiari, oh Dio! Ben chiari e tristi,
nel tuo dir presagi intendo!
Ah Lucia, Lucia desisti da un amor così
tremendo.

Alice:
Oh God! That vision of yours forebodes a
dark future!
Lucy, Lucy, end this disastrous love affair
that could become disastrous.

Lucia:
Egli è luce a' giorni miei,
è conforto al mio penar.

Lucy:
He is the light of my life.
He is the comfort of my pain.

Moderato
LUCY

Quando rapito in estasi
del più cocente ardore,
col favellar del core,
mi giura eterna fè.
Gli affanni miei dimentico,
gioia diviene il pianto,
parmi che a lui d'accanto
si schiuda il ciel per me!

I'm caught in the rapture
of his burning love.
With all his heart,
he has sworn to be true to me forever.
All my troubles are forgotten,
because my sorrow turns to joy.
When he is near to me,
it is as if heaven opened to me!

Alisa:
Ah! Giorni d'amaro pianto, s'apprestano
per te!

Alice:
What bitter days lie ahead for you!

Egli s'avanza!
La vicina soglia io cauta veglierò.

He is coming!
I'll be nearby, keeping watch.

Alice leaves. Edgar arrives.

Edgardo:
Lucia, perdona se ad ora inusitata io vederti
chiedea: ragion possente a ciò mi trasse.
Pria che in ciel biancheggi l'alba novella,
dalle patrie sponde lungi sarò.

Edgar:
Lucy, forgive me for calling you here at this
hour, but important duties call me.
Before dawn, in the early morning,
I will be far from our shores.

Lucia:
Che dici!

Lucy:
What are you saying!

Edgardo:
Pe' Franchi lidi amici sciolgo le vele:
ivi trattar m'è dato le sorti della Scozia.

Edgar:
I'm sailing to the friendly shores of France
to negotiate Scotland's future.

Lucia:
E me nel pianto abbandoni così!

Lucy:
And you abandon me like this!

Edgardo:
Pria di lasciarti Asthon mi vegga io stenderò
placato a lui la destra, e la tua destra, pegno
fra noi di pace, chiederò.

Edgar:
Before my departure I'll seek your brother. I'll
give him my hand in friendship, and I'll ask
for your hand as a sign of peace between us.

Lucia:
Che ascolto! Ah! no, rimanga nel silenzio
sepolto per or l'arcano affetto.

Lucy:
What am I hearing! No, let's let our love
remain a secret.

Edgardo:
Intendo!
Di mia stirpe il reo persecutore
de' mali miei ancor pago non è!
Mi tolse il padre, ill mio retaggio avito.
Né basta? Che brama ancor quel cor

Edgar: *(ironically)*
I understand now!
The man who persecuted my clan is not just
content with my misfortune!
He murdered my father and seized my
inheritance.

feroce e rio?
La mia perdita intera? Il sangue mio?
Egli m'odia!

Lucia:
Ah, no!

Edgardo:
Mi abborre!

Lucia:
Calma, oh ciel, quell'ira estrema!

Edgardo:
Fiamma ardente in sen mi corre! M'odi!

Lucia:
Edgardo!

Edgardo:
M'odi, e trema!
Sulla tomba che rinserra il tradito genitore,
al tuo sangue eterna guerra
io giurai nel mio furore:
ma ti vidi in cor mi nacque
altro affetto, e l'ira tacque.
Pur quel voto non è infranto,
io potrei compirlo ancor!

Lucia:
Deh! Ti placa, deh! Ti frena!
Può tradirne un solo accento!
Non ti basta la mia pena?
Vuoi ch'io mora di spavento?
Ceda, ceda ogn'altro affetto,
solo amor t'infiammi il petto;
un più nobile,più santo d'ogni voto
èun puro amor!

Edgardo:
Qui di sposa eterna fede,
qui mi giura, al cielo innante.
Dio ci ascolta, Dio ci vede;
tempio ed ara è un core amante;
al tuo fato unisco il mio:

What more does that vicious criminal want?
My very life? My blood?
He hates me!

Lucy:
No!

Edgar: *(more forcefully)*
He despises me!

Lucy:
Calm your extreme anger!

Edgar:
I'm inflamed with anger! Listen to me!

Lucy:
Edgar!

Edgar:
Hear me, and tremble!
On the grave of my poor, betrayed father,
I swore an oath of eternal revenge against
your family.
Then I saw you, and a new emotion stirred
my heart.
My anger abated. But I have not yet revoked
my vow. I could still carry it out!

Lucy:
Be calm! Restrain yourself!
A single word could give us away!
Isn't my anguish enough?
Do you want me to die of grief?
Put aside your anger and hatred.
Let love alone burn in your heart.
Nothing is more noble or holy than the vow
of pure love!

Edgar: *(with determination)*
Swear eternal loyalty to me as my bride.
Swear it, before Heaven.
God sees and hears us.
Our loving hearts shall be our temple.
And your destiny will be united with mine.

Edgar places his ring on Lucy's finger.

Son tuo sposo.

I am your husband.

Lucia:
E tua son io.

Lucy: *(gives her ring to Edgar)*
And I am your wife.

Lucia e Edgardo:
Ah! Soltanto il nostro foco spegnerà di morte il gel.
A' miei voti amore invoco, a' miei voto invoco il ciel.

Lucy and Edgar:
Only death will extinguish the flames of our love.
And only death can part us. I invoke heaven to guard us from all danger.

Edgardo:
Separaci omai conviene.

Edgar:
We must part now.

Lucia:
Oh parola a me funesta!
Il mio cor con te ne viene.

Lucy:
What sad words!
My heart will go with you.

Edgardo:
Il mio cor con te qui resta.

Edgar:
And my heart will remain here with you.

Lucia:
Ah! Edgardo! Ah! Edgardo!

Lucy:
Ah! Edgar! Ah! Edgar!

Edgardo:
Separci omai convien.

Edgar:
We will never be parted.

Lucia:
Ah! Talor del tuo pensiero venga un foglio messagiero,
e la vita fuggitiva di speranze nudrirò.

Lucy:
Let me know you are thinking of me. Send me your thoughts in a letter.
Hope will become my nourishment in life.

Edgardo:
Io di te memoria viva sempre, or cara, serberò.

Edgar:
I shall think of you always, my dearest.

Moderato assai
LUCY and EDGAR

Ver-ran - no a te sul - l'a - u - re   i miei so - spi-ri ar - den - te,

Lucia e Edgardo:
Ah! Veranno a te sull'aure
i miei sospiri ardenti,
udrai nel mar che mormora,
l'eco de' miei lamenti.

Lucy and Edgar:
The breeze will carry
my loving sighs to you.
And my laments will echo
in the murmuring seas.

Pensando ch'io di gemiti
mi pasco e di dolor,
spargi un'amara lagrima
su questo pegno allor.

Think of my pain
and my suffering.
Then shed a tear
on the vow of our love.

Edgardo:
Io parto.

Edgar:
I must leave.

Lucia:
Addio.

Lucy:
Farewell.

Edgardo:
Rammentati, ne stringe il ciel!

Edgar:
Remember, we are united by Heaven!

Lucia:
Edgardo!

Lucy:
Edgar!

Edgardo:
Addio!

Edgar:
Farewell!

Edgar departs. Lucy retires into the Castle.

Act II - Scene 1

"The Marriage Contract"

The apartments of Lord Henry Ashton in the Lammermoor castle.
Henry is seated beside a table, deep in thought.

Normanno:
Lucia fra poco a te verrà.

Norman:
Lucy will soon be here.

Enrico:
Tremante l'aspetto.
A festeggiar le nozze illustri,
già nel castello i nobili parenti
giunser di mia famiglia;
in breve Arturo qui volge.

Henry:
I'm anxiously waiting for her.
My noble kinsmen
are already here
to celebrate the wedding.
Soon, Arthur will arrive.

E s'ella pertinace osasse d'opporsi?

But what if Lucy continues to defy me?

Normanno:
Non temer: la lunga assenza del tuo nemico,
i fogli da noi rapiti, e la bugiarda nuova
ch'egli s'accese d'altra fiamma, in core
di Lucia spegneranno il cieco amore.

Norman:
Do not fear. Your enemy has been gone for a
very long time.
We've intercepted all of his letters to Lucy.
We'll make her believe he's in love with
another woman, and rid her of this blind
obsession.

Enrico:
Ella s'avanza!
Il simulato foglio porgimi.

Henry:
She is coming.
Give me the letter you forged.

Norman gives Henry the letter.

Ed esci sulla via che tragge
alla città regina di Scozia,
e qui fra plausi e liete grida conduci Arturo.

Now go to the main road that leads
to Edinburgh.
Escort Arthur here with all due ceremony.

Norman departs.

Lucy appears at the doorway. She hesitates, despondent and in anguish.

Enrico:
Appressati, Lucia.

Henry:
Come here to me, Lucy.

Lucy enters the room. She is extremely nervous and stares fixedly at her brother.

Sperai più lieta in questo dì vederti,
in questo dì, che d'imeneo le faci
s'accendono per te.
Mi guardi, e taci?

I hoped so see you looking happier today.
After all, the marriage torches are being lit
for you.
Why do you stare at me so silently?

Lucia:
Il pallor funesto orrendo,
che ricopre il volto mio,
ti rimprovero tacendo
il mio strazio, il mio dolore.
Perdonare ti possa Iddio
l'inumano tuo rigor!

Lucy:
You notice the terrible deathly pallor
that covers my face.
It accuses you as the cause
of my torture and pain.
Only God can forgive you
for your inhuman cruelty to me!

Enrico:
A ragion mi fe' spietato
quel che t'arse indegno affetto;
ma si taccia del passato;
tuo fratello, sono ancor.
Spenta è l'ira nel mio petto,
spegni tu l'insano amor.

Henry:
I had reason to be angry.
You had an affair with our clan's enemy.
But that is in the past now.
I am still your brother.
I have extinguished my anger.
Now put aside this insane love of yours.

Nobil sposo...

Your noble husband...

Lucia:
Cessa, cessa!

Lucy:
No more, no more!

Enrico:
Come?

Henry:
Why?

Lucia:
Ad altr'uomo giurai la fè.

Lucy:
I am pledged to another man.

Enrico:
Nol potevi.

Henry: *(angrily)*
You cannot do this.

Lucia:
Enrico!

Lucy:
Henry!

Enrico:
Nol potevi.

Henry:
You cannot do this.

Lucia:
Ad altro giurai mia fè.

Lucy:
I am pledged to another man.

Enrico:
Basti!

Henry: *(restraining his anger)*
Enough!

Henry gives Lucy the forged letter he received from Norman.

Questo foglio appien ti dice
qual crudel, qual empio amasti.
Leggi!

This letter will prove what a scoundrel you
loved.
Read it!

Lucy reads the letter. She becomes terrified, dismayed, and trembles.

Lucia:
Il core mi balzò!

Lucy:
My heart is breaking!

Enrico:
Tu vacilli!

Henry: *(rushing to assist her)*
You are trembling!

Lucia:
Me infelice! Ahi!
La folgore piombò!

Lucy:
What unhappiness!
The thunderbolt has struck!

Larghetto
LUCY

Soff - rir - va nel pianto, langui - a nel do - lo - re.

Soffriva nel pianto, languia nel dolore,
la speme, la vita riposi in un cor,
l'istante di morte è giunto per me!
Quel core infedele ad altra di diè!

What pain I suffered. What misery I
endured. I trusted my life to his love.
Now the hour of my death has arrived!
The unfaithful man loves another woman.

Enrico:
Un folle ti accese, un perfido amore;
tradisti il tuo sangue per vil seduttore,
ma degna dal cielo ne avesti mercé:
quel core infedele ad altra si diè!

Henry:
It was madness. He was a perfidious lover.
You betrayed your own family for a vile
seducer. Now merciful heaven has rescued
you. That betrayer loves another woman!

Festive music is heard from a hall in the castle.

Lucia:
Che fia?

Lucy:
What is that music?

Enrico:
Suonar di giubbilo, senti la riva.

Henry:
It is the sound of celebration.

Lucia:
Ebbene?

Lucy:
Why?

Enrico:
Giunge il tuo sposo.

Henry:
Your bridegroom has arrived.

Lucia:
Un brivido mi corse per le vene!

Lucy:
An icy chill overcomes me!

Enrico:
A te s'appresta il talamo.

Henry:
The nuptial hour approaches.

Lucia:
La tomba a me s'appresta!

Lucy:
Prepare my grave instead!

Enrico:
Ora fatale è questa!

Henry:
It is the fatal hour!

Lucia:
Ho sugli'occhi un vel!

Lucy:
My sight grows dim!

Enrico:
M'odi!
Spento è Guglielmo,
ascendere vedremo il trono Maria.
Prostrata è nella polvere
la parte ch'io seguia.

Henry:
Listen to me!
King William is dead.
Mary will ascend the throne.
The party I followed
has fallen from power.

Lucia:
Ah! Io tremo!

Lucy:
I am trembling!

Enrico:
Dal precipizio Arturo può sottrarmi,
sol egli.

Henry:
Only Arthur can rescue me from total ruin.

Lucia:
Ed io?

Lucy:
And what about me?

Enrico:
Salvarmi devi.

Henry:
You must save me.

Lucia:
Enrico!

Lucy:
Henry!

Enrico:
Vieni allo sposo!

Henry:
Go to your bridegroom!

Lucia:
Ad altri giurai.

Lucy:
But my oath.

Enrico:
Devi salvarmi. Il devi.

Henry:
You must save me. You must.

Lucia:
Oh ciel! Oh ciel!

Lucy:
Oh heavens!

Vivace
HENRY

Se - tra-dir - mi   tu   po - tra - i,   la   mia sorte è già com-pi - ta,

Enrico:
Se tradirmi tu potrai,
la mia sorte è già compita;
tu m'involi onore e vita,
tu la scure appresti a me.
Ne' tuoi sogni mi vedrai,
ombra irata e minacciosa!
Quella scure sanguinosa
starà sempre innanzi a te!

Henry: *(energetically)*
If you betray me,
my fate is sealed.
You'll rob me of my honor and my life.
You will wield the axe that decapitates me.
And I'll haunt your dreams,
like a furious, threatening ghost!
That bloodstained axe,
will follow you the rest of your life!

Lucia:
Tu che vedi il pianto mio,
tu che leggi in questo core,
se respinto il mio dolore,
come in terra, in ciel non è.
Tu mi togli, eterno Iddio,
questa vita disperata,
io son tanto sventurata,
che la morte è un ben per me!

Lucy: *(tearfully looking upwards)*
Lord. You see my tears.
You read my heart,
and you reject my pain.
As on earth, heaven does not exist.
Eternal God, take me away,
from this despairing life.
I am so unfortunate,
that death is a better fate for me!

Henry departs, as Lucy sinks into a chair.

Raymond Bidebent enters; he is a minister and Lucy's tutor.
Lucy anxiously hastens to meet him.

Lucia:
Ebben?

Lucy:
Is there any news?

Raimondo:
Di tua speranza l'ultimo raggio tramontò!
Credei , al tuo sospetto, che il fratel
chiudesse tutte le strade onde sul franco
suolo, all'uomo che amar giurasti,
non giungesser tue nuove:
io stesso un foglio da te vergato per secura
mano recar gli feci invano!
Tace mai sempre.
Quel silenzio assai d'infedeltà ti parla!

Raymond:
Your last hope has been crushed.
You suspected that your brother would stop
at nothing to keep your letters from reaching
the man you love in France.
So I gave one of your letters to a trusted
friend to deliver himself,
but it was useless.
There is no word from Edgar,
so his silence must mean that he is unfaithful!

Lucia:
E me consigli?

Lucy:
What is your advice?

Raimondo:
Di piegarti al destino.

Raymond:
Accept your fate.

Lucia:
E il giuramento?

Lucy:
What about my vow to him?

Raimondo:
Tu pur vaneggi!
I nuziali voti che il ministro di Dio non
benedice, nè il ciel, nè il mondo riconosce.

Raymond:
You're too delirious!
No minister of God blessed that marriage
vow, neither in Heaven, or on earth.

Lucia:
Ah! Cede persuasa la mente, ma sordo alla
ragion resiste il core!

Lucy:
Stop trying to persuade me. My heart resists
reason!

Raimondo:
Vincerlo è forza.

Raymond:
Force yourself to accept your fate.

Lucia:
Oh, sventurato amore!

Lucy:
Oh, what an unfortunate love!

Cantabile
RAYMOND

Ah!   Ce - di,   ce - di,   o più   scia - gu   -   re,

Raimondo:
Ah! Cedi, cedi, o più sciagure
ti sovrastano, infelice.
Per le tenere mie cure,
per l'estinta genitrice,
il periglio d'un fratello,
deh ti muova, e cangi il cor.
O la madre, nell'avello fremerà,
per te d'orror.

Lucia:
Taci, taci!

Raimondo:
No, no, cedi.

Lucia:
Ah! Ah! Taci.

Raimondo:
La madre, il fratello.

Lucia:
Ah! VIncesti.
Non son tanto snaturata.

Raimondo:
Oh! Qual gioia in me tu desti!
Oh qual nube hai dissipata!

Al ben de' tuoi qual vittima
offri, Lucia, te stessa;
e tanto sacrifizio
scritto nel ciel sarà.
Se la pietà degli uomini
a te non fia concessa,
v'è un Dio, v'è un Dio,
che tergere il pianto tuo saprà.

Lucia:
Guidami tu, tu reggimi,
son fuori di me stessa!
Lungo, crudel supplizio
la vita a me sarà!

Raymond:
Yield, or you'll suffer
an even worse disaster.
Think of the tender care
I've given you.
Think of your dead mother.
Think of the danger your brother is in.
Relent and change your mind, or your mother
will shudder with horror in her grave.

Lucy:
Quiet!

Raymond:
No, no, that is enough.

Lucy:
Quiet.

Raymond:
Your mother, your brother.

Lucy: *(conceding to Raymond)*
You've won.
I'm not that inhuman.

Raymond:
How happy you've made me!
The dark clouds have disappeared!.

You're sacrificing yourself for the good of
your family, Lucy.
And your deed
will be rewarded in Heaven.
Though you have received little mercy
from mankind,
there is a God who will give you comfort
and dry your tears.

Lucy:
Guide me, support me!
I am not in control of myself!
It is a profound sacrifice,
that has overcome my life!

Raymond departs.

Act II - Scene 2

The Great Hall of the Castle

*The hall has been prepared for a reception to honor the arrival of Lord Arthur Bucklaw
and perform the wedding of Lucy to Arthur.*

Moderato mosso
CHORUS

Per te d'immenso giu - bi - lo, tut - to s'avviva in - tor - no.

Enrico, Normanno, Coro:
Per te d'immenso giubilo
tutto s'avviva intorno,
per te veggiam rinascere
della speranza il giorno,
qui l'amistà ti guida,
qui ti conduce amore,
tutto ravviva intorno,
qui ti conduce amor,
qual astro in notte infida,
qual riso nel dolor.

Henry, Norman, Chorus:
We're gathered here in great joy.
Because of you,
our hopes
are renewed.
Here friendships guide us,
here love guides us.
All is bright around us,
and here love guides us.
from that unfaithful night star
that is like a smile of sorrow.

Arturo:
Per poco fra le tenebre
sparì la vostra stella:
io la farò risorgere
più fulgida, più bella.
La man mi porgi, Enrico,
ti stringi a questo cor,
a te ne vengo amico,
fratello e difensor.

Arthur: *(addressing Henry)*
Your star will rise again
out of the darkest clouds.
I will make it shine again,
more brightly and more beautiful.
Give me your hand, Henry.
I will embrace you with all my heart.
I come to you as a friend,
a brother, and a protector.

Dov'è Lucia?

Where is Lucy?

Enrico:
Qui giungere or la vedrem.

Henry:
She'll be here soon.

(Aside to Arthur)

Se in lei soverchia e la mestizia,
maravigliarti, no, no, non dei.
Dal duolo oppressa e vinta,
piange la madre estinta.

Don't be surprised if she seems overcome
by despair.
She is oppressed by grief,
and she is still in mourning for her mother.

Arturo:
M'è noto, sì, sì, m'è noto.

Arthur:
I understand well.

Enrico:
Soverchia e la mestizia, ma piange la
madre.

Henry:
She is overcome with despair,
and mourns for her mother.

Arturo:
Or solvi un dubbio.
Fama suonò, ch'Edgardo
sovr'essa temerario
alzare osò lo sguardo temerario.

Arthur:
Help me resolve a doubt.
I heard rumors about Edgar:
that he dared to court Lucy;
that he dared to look at her recklessly.

Enrico:
È vero, quel folle ardia, ma...

Henry:
True, he was wildly in love with her, but..

Arturo:
Ah!

Arthur:
Ah!

Normanno, Coro:
S'avanza qui Lucia.

Norman, Chorus:
Lucy is coming.

Enrico:
Piange la madre estinta.

Henry: *(to Arthur)*
Remember, she still mourns her mother.

*Lucy enters, accompanied by Raymond and Alice; she is melancholy and despondent.
Henry present Lucy to Arthur; she immediately withdraws from him.*

Enrico:
Ecco il tuo sposo.

Henry: *(to Lucy)*
Here is your bridegroom.

(Henry whispers to Lucy)

(Incauta! Perder mi vuoi?)

(Be careful! Do you want to destroy me?)

Lucia:
(Gran Dio!)

Lucy:
(Oh, God!)

Arturo:
Ti piaccia i voti accogliere del tenero amor
mio.

Arthur: *(to Lucy)*
Please accept my vow of tender love for
you.

Henry interrupts Arthur and proceeds to the table upon which the marriage contract lies.

Enrico:
(Incauta!)
Omai si compia il rito.
T'appressa.

Henry: *(aside to Lucy)*
(Be careful!)
Now sign the marriage contract.
It is prepared for you.

Lucia:　　　　　　　　　　　　　　　**Lucy:**
(Gran Dio!)　　　　　　　　　　　　　　(Oh, God!)

Arturo:　　　　　　　　　　　　　　　**Arthur:**
Oh dolce invito!　　　　　　　　　　　　Such a sweet conquest!

Arthur goes to the table and signs the marriage contract.
Raymond and Alice lead the trembling Lucy to the table.

Lucia:　　　　　　　　　　　　　　　**Lucy:**
(Io vado al sacrifizio! Me misera!)　　　　(I'm going to my sacrifice! What misery!)

　　　　　　　　　　　　　　　　　　(Lucy signs the marriage contract)
(La mia condanna ho scritta!)　　　　　　(I've signed my death warrant!)

Enrico:　　　　　　　　　　　　　　　**Henry:**
(Respiro!)　　　　　　　　　　　　　　　(I can breathe now!)

Lucia:　　　　　　　　　　　　　　　**Lucy:**
(Io gelo e ardo!　　　　　　　　　　　　(I'm freezing and I'm burning!)

Edgar enters from the door at the back of the hall,
causing an uproar from the wedding guests.

Tutti:　　　　　　　　　　　　　　　**All:**
Qual fragor!　　　　　　　　　　　　　What an uproar!
Chi giunge?　　　　　　　　　　　　　Who has arrived?

Edgardo:　　　　　　　　　　　　　　**Edgar:** *(in a terrifying voice)*
Edgardo!　　　　　　　　　　　　　　Edgar!

Tutti:　　　　　　　　　　　　　　　**All:**
Edgardo!　　　　　　　　　　　　　　Edgar!

Lucia:　　　　　　　　　　　　　　　**Lucy:**
Edgardo! Oh fulmine!　　　　　　　　　Edgar! What a thunderbolt!

Lucy faints and falls to the ground.

Tutti:　　　　　　　　　　　　　　　**All:**
Oh terror!　　　　　　　　　　　　　What a horror!

Alice, aided by some ladies, raises Lucy and leads her to a seat.

Alisa:　　　　　　　　　　　　　　　**Alice:**
Edgardo!　　　　　　　　　　　　　　Edgar!

Raimono e Coro:　　　　　　　　　　**Raymond and Chorus:**
Oh terror!　　　　　　　　　　　　　What a horror!

Larghetto
EDGAR and HENRY

EDGAR: *Chi mi fre - na in tal mo - me - to?*
What restrains me at this moment,

HENRY: *Chi raf - fre - na il mio fu - ro - re,*
What restrains my fury,

Enrico:

(Chi raffrena il mio furore,
e la man che al brando corse?
Della misera in favore
nel mio petto un grido sorse!
È il mio sangue! L'ho tradita!
Ella sta fra morte e vita!
Ah! Che spegnere non posso
i rimorso nel mio core!)

Henry: *(aside)*

(What restrains my furor
that I cannot raise my sword?
A dark misery screams
from the depths of my breast!
She is my own blood! I have betrayed her!
She is poised between life and death!
I cannot extinguish the remorse in my
heart!)

Edgardo:

(Chi mi frena in tal momento
chi troncò dell'ire il corso?
Il suo duolo, il suo spavento
son la prova d'un rimorso!
Ma, qual rosa inaridita,
ella sta fra morte e vita!
Io son vinto, son commosso!
T'amo, ingrata, t'amo ancor!)

Edgar:

(What restrains me in this moment
from venting my fury?
Her grief and fright
prove that she is guilty!
But that parched rose,
is poised between life and death!
I am defeated, and I am overwhelmed!
I still love you, unfaithful woman!)

Lucia:

(Io sperai che a me la vita
tronca avesse il mio spavento,
ma la morte non m'aita,
vivo ancor per mio tormento!
Da' miei lumi cadde il velo,
mi tradì la terra e il cielo!
Vorrei piangere, e non posso,
m'abbandona, il pianto ancor!)

Lucy:

(I was hoping my life would end,
and bring an end to my fears.
But death has not come to save me.
I still live and suffer!
Now I realize what has happened.
Both Heaven and earth have betrayed me!
I want to cry but I cannot.
The comfort of tears has been denied to me!)

Arturo, Raimondo, Alisa, Normanno, Coro:

(Qual terribile momento!
Più formar non so parole.
Densa nube di spavento
par che copra i rai del sole!
Come rosa, inaridita,
ella sta fra morte e vita!
Chi per lei non è commosso,
ha di tigre in petto il cor.)

Arthur, Raymond, Alice, Chorus:

(What a terrible moment!
I cannot find words.
Dense, dark clouds have gathered
and covered the rays of the sun!
Like a parched rose,
she is poised between life and death!
One who is not compassionate to her
has a tiger in his heart.)

Enrico, Arturo, Normanno, Cavalieri:
T'allontana sciagurato
o il tuo sangue fia versato.

Henry, Arthur, Norman, Cavaliers:
Leave, you wretch,
or your blood will be shed.

All rush toward Edgar with their swords brandished.

Edgardo:
Morirò, ma insiem col mio altro sangue
scorrerà.

Edgar: *(drawing his sword)*
I will die, but with my death, other blood
will flow.

Raimondo:
Rispettate in me di Dio la tremenda
maestà.
In suo nome io vel comando,
deponete l'ira e il brando.
Pace, pace, egli abborrisce l'omicida,
e scritto sta:
"Chi di ferro altrui ferisce,
pur di ferro perirà." Pace, pace.

Raymond: *(intervening authoritatively)*
Have respect for God's awesome majesty.
In His name, I order you
to put down your swords.
Peace! Peace! The Lord abhors murder,
and it is written:
"He who lives by the sword
shall die by the sword."
Peace, peace.

All sheathe their swords.

Enrico:
Sconsigliato!
In queste porte chi ti guida?

Henry: *(confronting Edgar)*
You are now discouraged!
What brought you to these portals?

Edgardo:
La mia sorte, il mio dritto.

Edgar: *(haughtily)*
My destiny, and my right.

Enrico:
Sciagurato!

Henry:
Scoundrel!

Edgardo:
Sì; Lucia la sua fede a me giurò!

Edgar:
Yes, Lucy pledged her love to me!

Raimondo:
Ah! Questo amor funesto obblia:
ella èd'altri!

Raymond:
That love is doomed.
She belongs to another.

Edgardo:
D'altri! No.

Edgar:
To another! No.

Raimondo:
Mira.

Raymond:
Look.

Raymond shows Edgar the marriage contract.
Edgar reads it quickly, and then eyes Lucy furiously.

Edgardo:
Tremi, ti confondi!
Son tue cifre?
A me rispondi:
Son tue cifre? Rispondi!

Edgar: *(to Lucy)*
You're trembling! You're humiliated!
Is this your writing?
Answer me!
Is this your writing? Answer me!

Lucia:
Sì!

Lucy: *(meekly)*
Yes!

Edgardo:
Riprendi il tuo pegno, infido cor.
Il mio dammi. Lo rendi.

Edgar: *(giving Lucy his ring)*
Take back your ring, unfaithful woman.
Give me mine. Return it.

Lucia:
Almen, Edgardo! Edgardo!.

Lucy:
If only, Edgar! Edgar!

Lucy, in her anguish, is totally confused.
She takes off her ring, which Edgar brusquely snatches from her.

Edgardo:
Hai tradito il cielo e amor!

Edgar:
You have betrayed both love and Heaven!

Maledetto sia l'istante
che di te mi rese amante,
stirpe iniqua, abbominata io dovea da te
fuggir!
Ah! Ma di Dio la mano irata
vi disperda.

I curse the moment
I began to love you.
I should have fled from this abominable
family.
But the angry hand of God will disperse
you.

Enrico, Arturo, Normanno, Cavalieri:
Insano ardir!
Esci, fuggi il furor che accende
solo un punto i suoi colpi sospende,
ma fra poco più atroce, più fiero
sul suo capo abborrito cadrà.

Henry, Arthur, Norman, Cavaliers:
Insane passion!
Leave! Flee from the fury
that has now inflamed us.
Soon something monstrous and more fierce
will fall upon your head.

Edgardo:
Trucidatemi, e pronubo al rito sia,
io scempio d'un core tradito.
Del mio sangue coperta la soglia;
dolce vista per l'empia sarà!
Calpestando l'esangue mia spoglia
all'altare più lieta se ne andrà!

Edgar:
Kill me now. My bleeding heart is the
wedding gift from a betrayed fool.
My blood covering the ground
will be a sweet sight for that wicked one!
She will trample on my blood as she walks
the path to the altar!

Lucia:
Dio lo salva, in sì fiero momento,
d'una misera ascolta l'accento.
È la prece d'immenso dolore
che più in terra speranza non ha.
E l'estrema domanda del core,
che sul labbro spirando mi sta!

Lucy:
May God save him!
It is a fierce and stressful moment.
It is the price of immense sorrow
that on earth there is no longer hope.
I am doomed to misery,
but do not refuse my last, dying prayer!

Arturo:
Va col sangue tuo lavata sarà.
Esci, fuggi!
Il furor che m'accende
solo un punto i suoi colpi sospende,
ma fra poco più atroce,
fiero sul tuo capo abborrito cadrà,
la macchia d'oltraggio
sì nero col tuo sangue lavata sarà!

Raimondo, Alisa, Dame:
Infelice! Deh ti salva!
Vivi, forse il tuo duolo fia spento,
tutto è lieve, all'eterna pietà,
infelice, t'invola, t'affretta, i tuoi giorni, il
suo stato rispetta, quante volte ad un solo
tormento, mille gioie apprestate non ha!

Arthur:
Go and your blood will be cleansed.
Leave, flee!
Flee from the fury
that has now inflamed us,
Soon something monstrous and more fierce
will fall upon your head.
It will be the mark of a dark tragedy,
and your blood will be cleansed!

Raymond, Alice, Women:
Unfortunate one! Save yourself!
Live, perhaps your sorrow has ended.
Everything is eased by Heavenly mercy.
flee, hurry, restore your self respect
and rank. How often a single torture is
succeeded by a thousand joys!

ACT III - Scene 1

A room in the Tower of Wolf's Crag. It is night, and a storm rages.
Edgar is seated by a table, immersed in thought.
After a few moments, he rises, goes to the window, and stares outside.

Edgardo:
Orrida è questa notte come il destino mio!

Edgar:
This night is as horrible as my destiny!

(Thunder is heard)

Sì, tuona, o cielo imperversate, o fulmini,
sconvolto sia l'ordin di natura e pera il
mondo!
Ma io non mi inganno!
Scalpitar d'appresso odo un destrier!
S'arresta!
Chi mai nella tempesta fra le minacce e
l'ira, chi puote a me venire?

Yes, the roar of raging heaven, and lightning.
The order of nature is overturned, as well as
the light of the world!
But if I am not mistaken!
I hear the sound of a rider!
He is stopping!
Who would come here amidst this
menacing storm?

Lord Henry Ashton enters, and immediately removes his cloak.

Enrico:
Io!

Henry:
I!

Edgardo:
Quale ardire! Asthon!

Edgar:
What boldness! Ashton!

Enrico:
Sì.

Henry:
Yes.

Edgardo:
Fra queste mura osi offrirti al mio cospetto!

Edgar:
You dare present yourself within these walls!

Enrico:
Io vi sto per tua sciagura.

Henry:
I am here because of your misfortune.

Edgardo:
Per mia?

Edgar:
For mine?

Enrico:
Non venisti nel mio tetto?

Henry:
Didn't you come to my home?

Moderato
EDGAR

Qui del pa - dre ancor-re - spi - ra   l'ombra inulta, e par che fre - ma!

Edgardo:
Qui del padre ancor respira,
l'ombra inulta, e par che frema!
Morte ogn'aura a te qui spira!
Il terren per te qui trema!
Nel varcar la soglia orrenda
ben dovresti palpitar,
come un uom che vivo scenda
la sua tomba ad albergar!

Edgar:
Here my father still breathes,
his ghost shuddering!
Death is in the air you breathe!
Here the earth shakes and trembles!
When you crossed the threshold
you were throbbing,
like a man descending
into his final tomb!

Enrico:
Fu condotta la sacro rito quindi al talamo
Lucia.

Henry: *(with savage joy)*
It was because of a sacred duty: the nuptial
bed of Lucy.

Edgardo:
(Ei più squarcia il cor ferito!
Oh tormento! Oh gelosia!)

Edgar:
(Another slice of a wounded heart!
What torment! What jealousy!)

Enrico:
Ella è al talamo.

Henry:
She is in her nuptial bed.

Edgardo:
(Oh gelosia!) Ebben? Ebben?

Edgar:
(What jealousy!) What more?

Enrico:
Ascolta!
Di letizia il mio soggiorno
e di plausi rimbombava;
ma più forte al cor d'intorno
la vendetta a me parlava!
Qui mi trassi, in mezzo ai venti,
la sua voce udia tuttor;
e il furor degl'elementi
rispondeva al mio furor!

Edgardo:
Da me che brami?

Enrico:
Ascoltami!
Onde punir l'offesa,
de' miei, la spada vindice
pende su te sospesa,
ch'altri ti spenga,
mai, chi dee svenarti il sai!

Edgardo:
So che al paterno cenere giurai strapparti
al core.

Edrico:
Tu!

Edgardo:
Quando?

Enrico:
Al primo sorgere del mattutino albore.

Edgardo:
Ove?

Enrico:
Fra l'urne gelide di Ravenswood.

Edgardo:
Verrò.Sì, verrò, sì, sì!

Enrico:
Ivi a restar preparati.

Edgardo:
Ivi t'ucciderò.

Henry:
Listen!
Joy and happiness have been thundering
around me,
and strengthened my heart,
because vengeance speaks to me!
I was drawn here, amidst a storm,
hearing your voice,
and the fury of the elements
increased my own fury!

Edgar: *(with haughty impatience)*
What do you want from me?

Henry:
Listen to me!
My sword will punish the
wrongs you committed against me.
I challenge you to a duel,
because nothing else can
erase your debauchery!

Edgar:
By the ashes of my father, I will
drain blood from your heart.

Henry:
You!

Edgar: *(with disdain)*
When shall we meet?

Henry:
At early dawn tomorrow.

Edgar:
Where?

Henry:
By the cold tombs of Ravenswood.

Edgar:
Yes, I will be there!

Henry:
Prepare yourself for death.

Edgar:
I will kill you there.

Enrico:
Al primo albrore.

Henry:
At early dawn.

Edgardo:
Al primo albore.

Edgar:
At early dawn.

Edgardo e Enrico:
Ah! O sole più ratto a sorger t'appresta,
ti cinga di sangue, ghirlanda funesta,
con quella rischiara l'orribile gara
d'un odio mortale, d'un cieco furore.
Giurai strappar tu cuore!

Edgar and Henry:
Hurry early sun, so I can surround him
with blood and a deadly garland.
I will risk this horrendous duel
of mortal hatred and blind fury.
I swear I will rip out your heart!

Enrico:
La spada pende su te.

Henry:
My sword awaits you.

Edgardo:
Fra l'urne di Ravenswood.

Edgar:
Among the urns of Ravenswood.

Enrico:
All'albe verro.

Henry:
At early morning.

Act III - Scene 2

A Hall at the Castle of Ravenswood. From adjoining rooms,
dance music is heard. Guests are conversing intimately.

Coro:
D'immenso giubilo
s'innalzi un grido,
di vivo giubbilo
corra di Scozia di lido,
e avverta i perfidi
nostri nemici.

Chorus:
Shouts of immense joy
have swelled on this happy day.
Buoyant exultation
comes from Scotland's shores.
We have averted the betrayal
of our enemies.

Che più terribili,
che piu felici,
ne rende l'aura
d'alto favor;
le stelle ancor!
Che a noi sorridono
le stelle ancor.

How terrible,
yet how joyful.
The star shines on us,
like the breath
of a Divine gift!
May the stars
always smile upon us.

Raimondo:
Cessi, ahi cessi quel contento!

Raymond:
Stop this celebration!

Coro:
Sei cosparso di pallore!
Ciel! Che rechi?

Chorus:
You seem pale!
Heavens! What has happened?

Raimondo:
Un fiero evento!

Raymond:
Something ghastly has happened!

Coro:
Tu ne agghiacci di terror!

Chorus:
You seem terrified and frightened!

Raimondo:

Raymond:
(Calling all to gather around him.)

Dalle stanze, ove Lucia
Tratta avea col suo consorte,
un lamento, un grido uscia,
come d'uom vicino a morte!

Lucy had retired to her rooms with her
husband.
I heard a scream; the cry of a man near
death.

Corsi ratto in quelle mura.
Ahi! Terribile sciagura!
Steso Arturo al suol giaceva,
nuto, freddo, insanguinato!
E Lucia l'acciar stringeva,
che fu già del trucidato!

I rushed into their chamber.
What a horrible sight!
Arthur lay on the floor, mute, cold, and
covered with blood.
Lucy was still holding the dagger over the
murdered man!

Ella in me le luci affisse:
"Il mio sposo, ov'è?" Mi disse:
e nel volto suo pallente
un sorriso balenò! Infelice!
Della mente la virtude a lei mancò!

She fixed her eyes on me:
"Where is my bridegroom?" She said.
And a smile flashed over her pale face.
Unfortunate woman!
She had lost her mind!

Tutti:
Oh! Qual funesto avvenimento!
Tutti ne ingombra cupo spavento!
Notte, ricopri la ria sventura
col tenebroso tuo denso vel.
Ah! Quella destra di sangue impura
l'ira non chiami su noi del ciel.

All:
What dreadful news!
We're all confounded and frightened!
Let night hide this misfortune
and cover us with its dark veil.
Heaven, do not let her bloodstained hand
bring Your wrath upon us all.

Raimond:
Ella in me la luci affisse, e lacciar stringeva!

Raymond:
Her eyes were blank, the dagger in her hand!

Eccola!

Here she is!

Lucy enters. She is wearing a plain white dress; her hair is dishevelled
and she is deathly pale. She is out of her senses and lost all touch with reality.

Coro:
(Oh giusto cielo! Par dalla tomba uscita!)

Chorus:
Oh Heaven! She looks like she's risen from the tomb!)

Lucia:
Il dolce suono mi colpì di sua voce!
Ah! quella voce m'è qui nel cor discesa!
Edgardo! Io ti son resa:
fuggita io son da' tuoi nemici.

Lucy:
The sweet sound of his voice struck me.
That voice of his pierced my heart.
Edgar! I am yours again.
I have escaped form your enemies.

Un gelo mi serpeggia nel sen!
Trema ogni fibra! Vacilla il piè!
Presso la fonte meco t'assidi alquanto!

What an icy chill runs through me!
My whole body is shaking.
Sit with me by the fountain for a while!

Ohimé! Sorge il tremendo fantasma e ne separa!
Ohimè! Ohimè! Edgardo! Edgardo!
Ah! Il fantasma ne separa!
Qui ricovriamo, Edgardo, a piè dell'ara.

That horrible ghost is rising up and driving us apart!
Alas! Edgar!
The ghost is driving us apart!
Edgar, Let's find a refuge.

Sparsa è di rose!Un'armonia celeste,
di', non ascolti?
Ah! L'inno suona di nozze!
Il rito per noi, per noi s'appresta!
Oh me felice!
Oh gioia che si sente, e non si dice!

Here's our wedding altar, scattered with roses! Do you hear the heavenly music?
It is the sound of our wedding hymn!
This is our marriage ceremony!
Oh, I'm so happy!
What joy I feel!

Ardon gl'incensi.
Splendon le sacre, splendon intorno!
Ecco il ministro!
Porgimi la destra!
Oh lieto giorno!
Alfin son tua, alfin sei mio, a me ti dona un Dio!.

They're lighting the incense.
The sacred wedding torches are glowing!
Here is the minister!
Give me your hand!
What a happy day!
At last I am yours, at last you are mine,
Heaven itself has given you to me!

Normanno, Raimondo, Alisa, Coro:
Abbi in sì crudo stato di lei,
Signore, di lei pietà.

Norman, Raymond, Alice, Chorus:
How horrifying she is.
God, mercy on her.

Lucia:
Ogni piacer più grato,
sì, mi fia con te diviso.
Del ciel clemente, un riso
la vita a noi sarà!

Lucy:
Every pleasure in life will be greater,
when it is shared with you.
How kind Heaven is, our life together
will be like a smile!

Raimondo:
S'avanza Enrico!

Raymond:
Henry is coming!

Enrico:
Ditemi: vera è l'atroce scena?

Raimondo:
Vera, pur troppo!

Enrico:
Ah! Perfida! Ne avrai condegna pena!

Normanno, Alisa, Coro:
T'arresta!

Raimondo:.
Oh ciel!
Non vedi lo stato suo?

Lucia:
Che chiedi?

Enrico:
Oh,qual pallor!
Gran Dio!

Lucia:
Ah, me misera!

Raimondo:
Ha la ragion smarrita.
Tremare, o barbaro,
Tu dei per la sua vita.

Lucia:
Non mi guardar sì fiero,
Segnai quel foglio, è vero.
Nell'ira sua terribile
Calpesta, oh Dio, l'anello!
Mi maledice!Ah!
Vittima fui d'un crudel fratello,
ma ognor t'amai, ognora, Edgardo,
sì, ognor t'amai, e t'amo ancor,
Edgardo mio, sì, te lo giuro,
t'amai e t'amo ancor!

Gli Altri:
Pietà di lei, Signor, pietà!

Lucia:
Chi mi nomasti?

Henry: *(rushing in)*
Tell me, is it true Arthur was murdered?

Raymond:
It is very true!

Henry: *(looking toward Lucy)*
Betrayer! You'll pay for this!

Norman, Alice, Chorus:
Contain yourself!

Raymond:
Oh Heaven!
Don't you see her condition?

Lucy:
What do you want?

Henry: *(deliriously)*
How pallid she is!
Great God!

Lucy:
I am so wretched!

Raymond:
She has lost her reason.
Tremble, heartless man.
You are responsible for this.

Lucy:
Don't look at me so angrily.
I signed that paper, it's true.
He was so infuriated.
He threw down our wedding ring.
And he cursed me.
But I was only the victim of a cruel brother.
I swear I have always loved you, Edgar.
I always loved you, and I still love you.
My Edgar, yes, I swear to you,
I love you and still love you!

The Others:
Mercy on her!

Lucy:
What name did you say?

Arturo! Tu nomasti. Arturo!	Arthur? You are Arthur!
Ah! Non fuggir! Ah, per pietà, perdon!	Don't leave, Edgar! Forgive me!
Ah! No, non fuggir, Edgardo!	No, don't leave, Edgar!

Gli Altri:
Qual notte di terror.

The Others:
What a horrible night!

Moderato

LUCY

Spar - gi d'a - ma - ro pian - to,
Spread your bitter tears

il mio ter - re - stre ve - lo,
over my earthly remains.

Lucia:
Spargi d'amaro pianto
il mio terrestre velo,
mentre lassù nel cielo
io pregherò per te.
Al giunger tuo soltanto
fia bello il ciel per me!

Lucy:
Spread your bitter tears
over my earthly remains.
In Heaven above,
I'll pray for you.
Only when you join me
will Heaven seem beautiful to me!

Enrico:
Giorni d'amaro pianto serba il rimorso a me.

Henry:
It is a day of bitter tears that has made me remorseful.

Raimond e Coro:
Piu raffrenare il pianto possibile non è!

Raymond and Chorus:
It is impossible for me to restrain my tears!

Enrico:
Sì tragga altrove. Alisa.

Uom del Signor, deh! Voi la misera vegliate.

Io più me stesso in me non trovo!

Henry:
Remove her carefully, Alice.
(to Raymond)
Man of God, look at this misery!

(Alice and ladies lead Lucy away)
I will only have remorse in my life!

Raimond:
Delator! Gioisci dell'opra tua!

Raymond: *(to Norman)*
Man of blood! Exult in your work!

Normanno:
Che parli?

Norman:
What are you saying?

Raimondo:
Sì, dell'incendio che divampa e strugge
questa casa infelice,
hai tu destata la primiera scintilla!

Raymond:
It was your hand that incited the crime and
created this unhappiness.
You sparked and kindled the flames!

Normanno:
Io non credei...

Norman:
I didn't believe...

Raimondo:
Tu del versato sangue, empio,
tu sei la ria cagion!
Quel sangue al ciel t'accusa,
e già la man suprema
segna la tua sentenza!
Or vanne, e trema!

Raymond:
You are the author of this crime. Traitor!
You are the reason!
For that blood, Heaven accuses you.
And already the hand of God
signs your sentence!
Go from here, and tremble!

Raymond follows Lucy. Norman exits.

ACT III - Scene 3

Outside the Castle of Wolf's crag. In the distance, an illuminated Hall.
It is the Tombs of Ravenswood at night.

Edgardo:
Tombe degli avi miei, l'ultimo avanzo
d'una stirpe infelice,
Deh! Raccogliete voi.

Edgar:
Tomb of my forefathers, receive the last
remains of our unhappy family.
Yes, gather the remains.

Cessò dell'ira il breve foco;
sul nemico acciaro abbandonar mi vo'.
Per me la vita è orrendo peso!
L'universo intero è un deserto per me senza
Lucia!
Di faci tutttavia splende il castello!
Ah! Scarsa fu la notte al tripudio!
Ingrata donna!
Mentr'io mi struggo in disperato pianto,
tu ridi, esulti accanto
al felice consorte!
Tu delle gioie in seno, io della morte!

This brief, angry struggle will soon end:
I will throw myself upon the enemy's sword.
Life has become a horrible burden for me!
Without Lucy, the entire world seems like a
desert to me!
The castle is still ablaze with torches!
The night is brief for those who celebrate!
Ungrateful woman!
While I am destroyed by despair and
anguish you rejoice by the side of your
happy husband!
You are filled with joy, and I with death!

Larghetto
EDGAR

Fra po - co a me ri - co - vero da - rà negletto a - vel - lo,

Fra poco a me ricovero darà negletto avello,	Soon I'll find refuge in a forgotten tomb.
una pietosa lagrima	No one will ever shed a tear of sorrow upon
non scendera su quello!	it!
Fin degli estinti, ahi misero!	In the end only death. Oh what misery!
Manca il conforto a me.	Even in death, I'll find no comfort!
Tu pur, tu pur dimentica	You, too, you will forget
quel marmo dispregiato:	my marble tomb.
mai non passarvi, o barbara,	Never come near it, heartless woman,
del tuo consorte a lato.	when your husband is at your side.
Ah! Rispetta almen le ceneri	At least respect the ashes
di chi moria per te!	of the man who died for you!

Voices are heard in the distance, coming from the Ashton Castle.

Coro:
Oh meschina! Oh fato orrendo!
Più sperar non giova omai!.
Questo dì che sta sorgendo
tramontar tu non vedrai!

Chorus:
The unhappy woman!. The horrible fate!
There is no hope left!
She has not lived
to see the dawn of a new day.

Edgardo:
Giusto cielo! Rispondete:
Di chi mai, di chi piangete?

Edgar:
For Heaven's sake! Tell me.
For whom do you mourn?

Coro:
Di Lucia.

Chorus:
For Lucy.

Edgardo:
Lucia diceste!

Edgar: *(stricken by terror).*
You said Lucy!

Coro:
Sì la misera sen muore.
Fur le nozze a lei funeste,
di ragion la trasse amore,
s'avvicina all'ore estreme,
e te chiede, per te geme.

Chorus:
The unfortunate woman died.
The wedding was fatal for her.
Her love for you robbed her of her senses.
Now her final hour approaches,
and she calls for you.

Edgardo:
Ah! Lucia! Lucia!.

Edgar:
Ah! Lucy! Lucy!

In the distance, the sound of death bells.

Coro:
Rimbomba già la squilla in suon di morte!

Chorus:
The death knell is already tolling!

Edgardo:
Quel suono al cor mi piomba!
È decisa la mia sorte!
Rivederla ancor vogl'io,
rivederla e poscia.

Edgar:
That sound pierces my heart!
It rings for me as well!
I want to see her again,
to see her after her death.

(Rushing off)

Coro:
Oh Dio
Qual trasporto, sconsigliato!.
Ah, desisti! Ah, riedi in te!

Chorus: *(trying to detain him)*
Oh, God!
That procession!
Stop!

Edgar is halted by Raymond.

Raimondo:
Dove corri, sventurato?
Ella in terra più non è.

Raymond:
Where are you going, unhappy man?
She is no longer in this world.

Edgardo:
Lucia!

Edgar:
Lucy!

Raimondo:
Sventurato!

Raymond:
It is unfortunate!

Edgardo:
In terra piu non è? Ella dunque.

Edgar:
Lucy is no longer in this world?

Raimondo:
È in cielo.

Raymond:
She is in Heaven.

Edgardo:
Lucia piu non è!

Edgar:
Lucy is dead!

Coro:
Svenurato!

Chorus:
It is unfortunate!

Moderato
EDGAR

Tu che a Dio spiega - sti l'a-li,   o bel - l'alma innamo - ra - ta.

Edgardo:
Tu che a Dio spiegasti l'ali,
o bell'alma innamorata,
ti rivolgi a me placata,
teco ascenda il tuo fedel.
Ah! Se l'ira dei mortali
fece a noi sì cruda guerra,
se divisi fummo in terra,
ne congiunga il Nume in ciel!

Edgar:
Now you will unfold your wings before
God, my beloved angel.
Lean down to embrace me serenely.
Your true love will join you.
We were caught in a fatal hatred
that became a cruel battle.
We were kept apart on earth,
Now may God unite us in Heaven!

Edgar grabs a dagger.

Io ti seguo.

I will follow you.

All try in vain to disarm him.

Raimondo:
Forsennato!

Raymond:
You are insane!

Raimond e Coro:
Ah! Che fai!

Raymond and Chorus:
What are your doing!

Edgardo:
Morir voglio.

Edgar:
I want to die.

Raimondo e Coro:
Ritorna in te.

Raymond and Chorus:
Give it to me.

Edgardo:
No, no, no!

Edgar:
No, no, no!

Edgar stabs himself.

Raimondo e Coro:
Ah! Che facesti!

Raymond and Chorus:
What have you done!

Edgardo:
A te vengo, o bell'alma, ti rivolgi, al tuop
fedel.
Ah se l'ira dei mortali si cruda guerra,
bell'alma, ne congiunga il Nume in cielo.

Edgar:
I am joining you, my lovely spirit. Your true
love will join you.
We were caught in a cruel battle,
My beloved, God will unite us in Heaven.

Raimondo e Coro:
Qual orror! Oh Dio perdona.
Pensa al ciel.
Dio, perdona tanto orror.

Raymond and Chorus:
What a horror! God forgive him.
Think of Heaven.
God, forgive this horror.

Edgar dies.

71893436R00024

Made in the USA
Columbia, SC
11 June 2017